TIM JEFFS ART
Animal Sketches
*Song*Birds

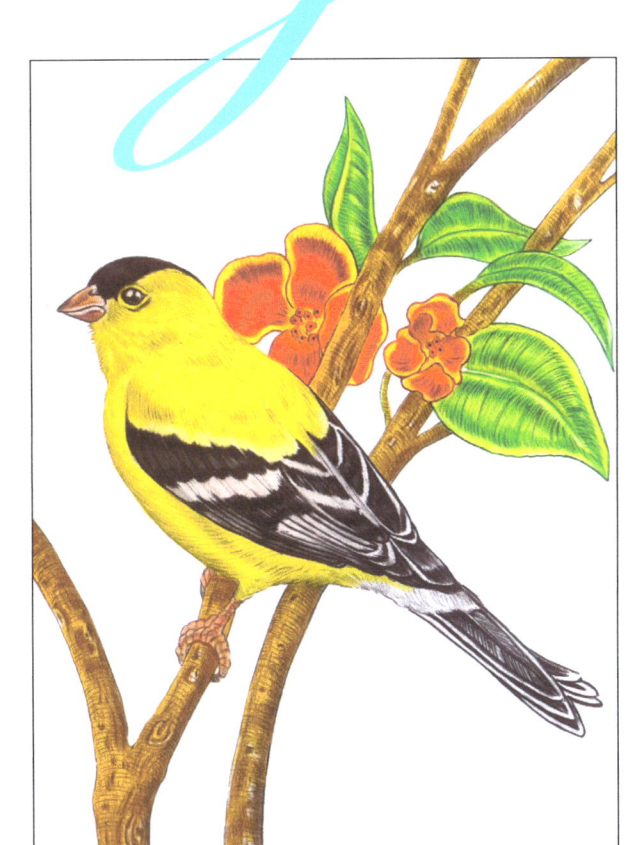

A Special Edition Coloring Book

For Jane, Jenna and Harrison

Dedicated to all of the wonderful colorists who have supported my art and made my drawings more beautiful with their colors, and all the precious creatures that we live among.
A special thank you to Jo Warren for all of her continued support and beautiful colorings and lesson that make this book so much more special!

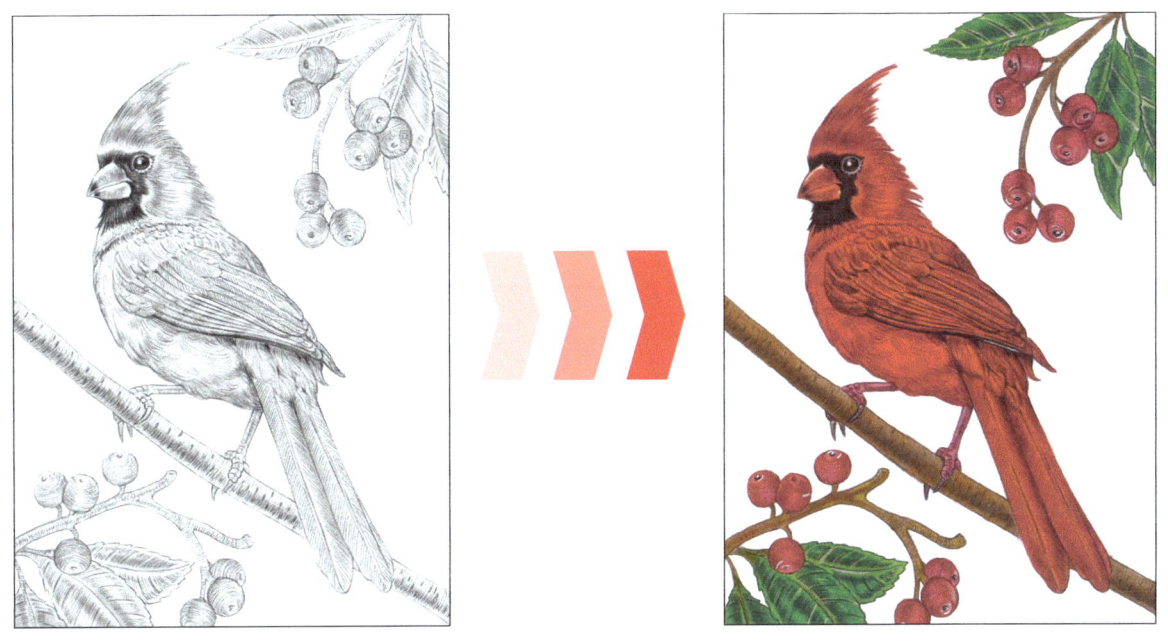

© Copyright 2021 Tim Jeffs Art
All rights reserved. No part of this publication may be reproduced or distributed in any form without the prior written permission of Tim Jeffs Art.

Tim Jeffs Art
376 East Madison Avenue, Dumont, NJ 07628

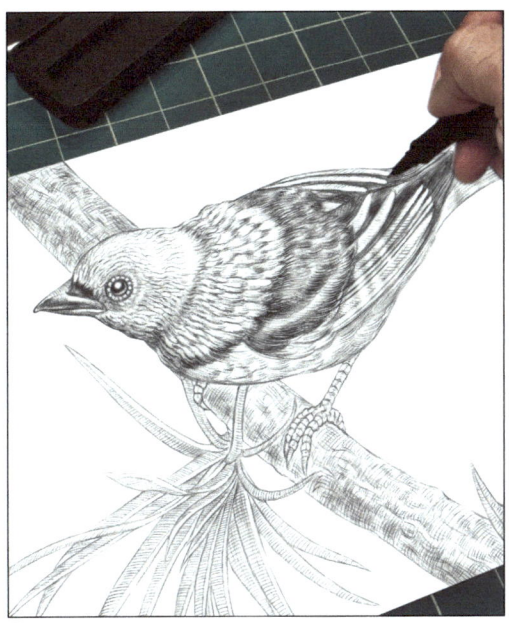 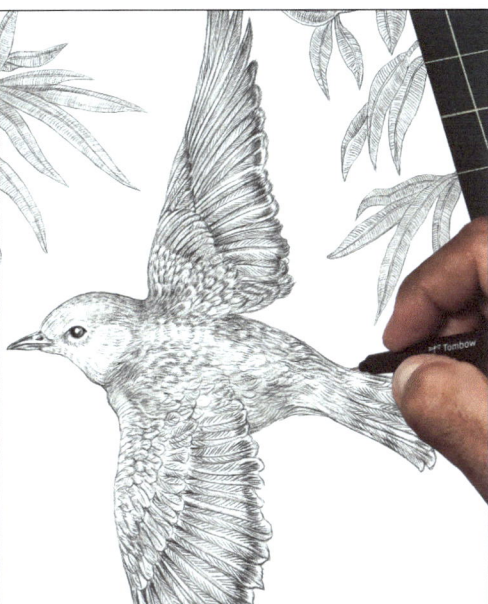 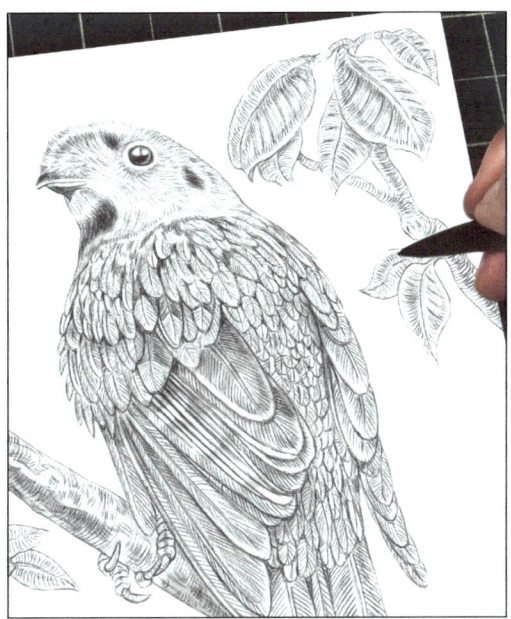

Song Birds Sketches Thoughts

Lovely songs, welcoming sights, and beautiful colors. Song birds consist of 5000 or so species found all over the world. They make up nearly half the worlds birds, and to me a walk in nature isn't the same without the wonderful sound of song birds singing around you. Birds are a very favorite drawing subject of mine, and like so many bird lovers and admirers seeing or hearing a new bird that you have never seen or heard before is a very exciting moment. I will continue to draw our feathered friends with great enthusiasm. Their endless intricate details, their wonderful sizes and shapes and their spectrum of fantastic colors always deliver so much drawing fun!

In this coloring book I've drawn my song birds among plants, flowers and vegetation which I hope will give you further coloring creativity options to have fun with.

I hope you enjoy coloring this group of song bird sketches as much as I enjoyed drawing them, and I know that with your colors, you will bring these beautiful birds and the plants they live among to life!

GRAYSCALE COLORING LESSON
Baltimore Oriole

Lesson level: Moderate

Coloring the Baltimore Oriole

On the next page I will walk you through the coloring of the Baltimore Oriole which is on page 2 of this coloring book. I've always enjoyed surprised visits to my yard by these gorgeous birds. It doesn't happen very often and they are always such a delight to see. This beautiful coloring of the Baltimore Oriole was done by Jo Warren. Many thanks for her creative and inspirational step-by-step photos in the coloring lesson.

❯ Supply List

In this lesson, Tombow Irojiten pencils were used, (pencil numbers are listed below) but you can use any brand with similar colors.

1) **The coloring page can be found on page 2**
2) **Colors: Towbow Irojiten pencils:**

Bird
V-3 Dandelion
V-2 Tangerine Orange
D-9 Mulberry – Dark Feathers
V-10 Ivory Black

Flowers
P-1 Orchid pink
P-2 Coral Pink
V-1 Cherry Red
V-3 Dandelion
V-2 Tangerine Orange
White gel pen

Legs
DL- 7 Jay Blue
P-10 Pigeon Grey

Leaves and Tree Trunk
P-5 Lettuce Green
V-5 Parrot Green
D-2 Chestnut Brown
D-4 Maple Sugar

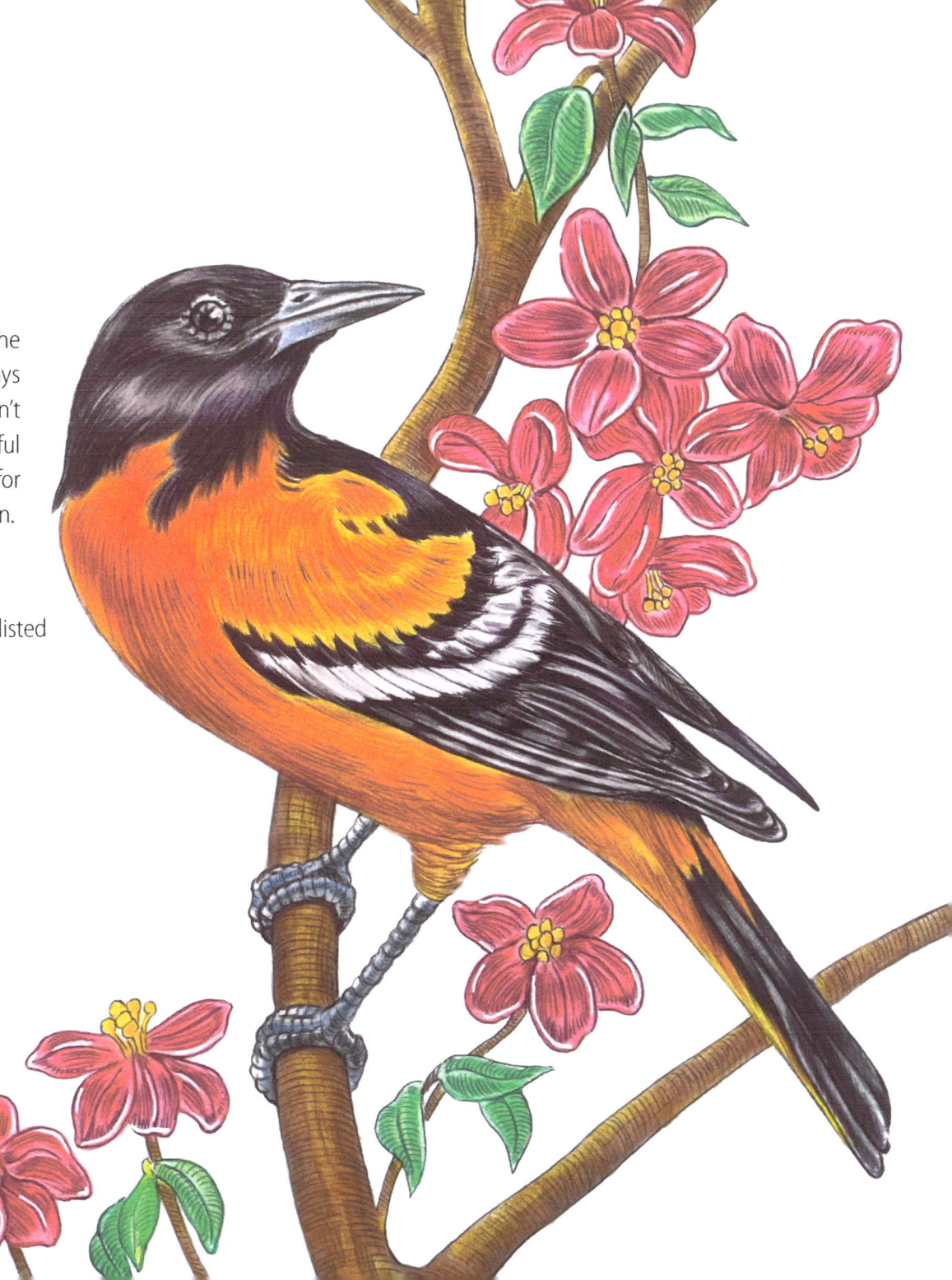

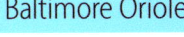

GRAYSCALE COLORING LESSON
Baltimore Oriole

Baltimore Oriole

Supplies needed: A variety of colorful pencils and a gel pen

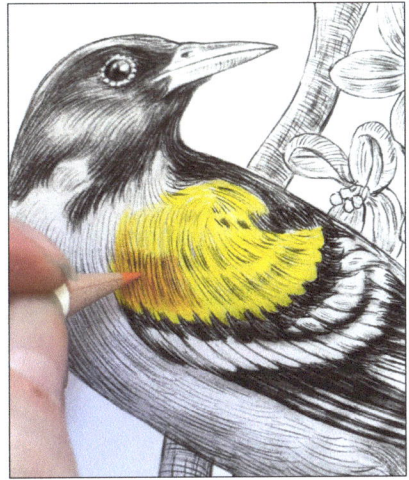

Step 1. Begin by coloring in the lighter areas of the Oriole's wing with Dandelion (V-3) and layer Tangerine Orange (V-2) on top leaving some of the yellow to show through. Especially next to the dark feathers.

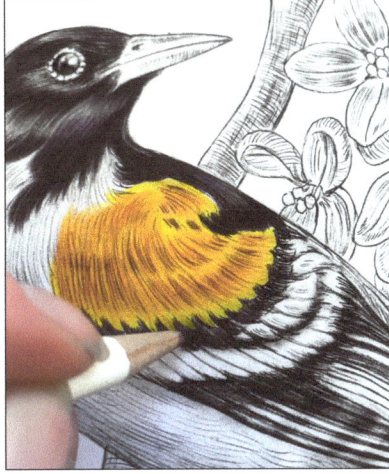

Step 2. Color over the dark feathers of the wing with (D-9) Mulberry and edge the feathers with (V-10) Ivory Black to give the feathers shape and depth. Repeat this step on the Oriole's head and tail feathers.

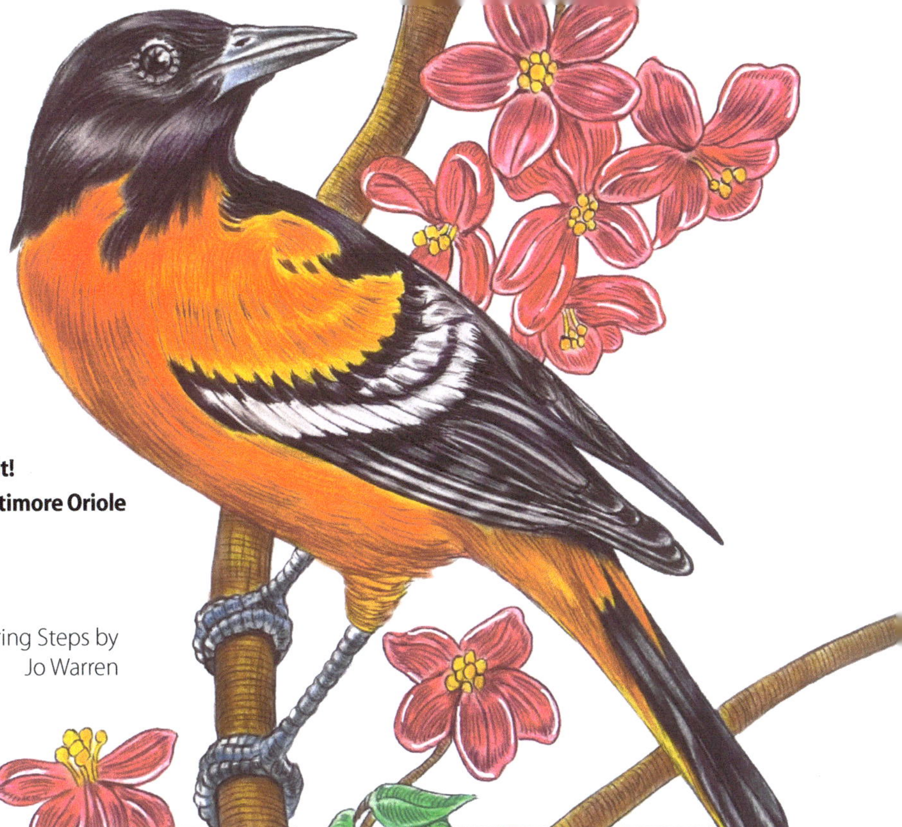

You did it! Your Baltimore Oriole is done!

Coloring Steps by Jo Warren

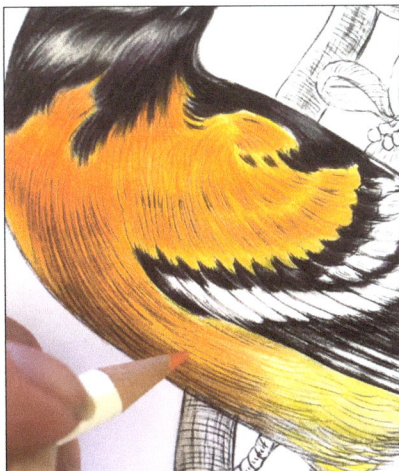

Step 3. Continue coloring the neck and body layering first (V-3) and then (V-2) on top. Make your orange deeper by coloring over it several times. Color over the white feathers in the wing with a white gel pen to lighten the feathers even more.

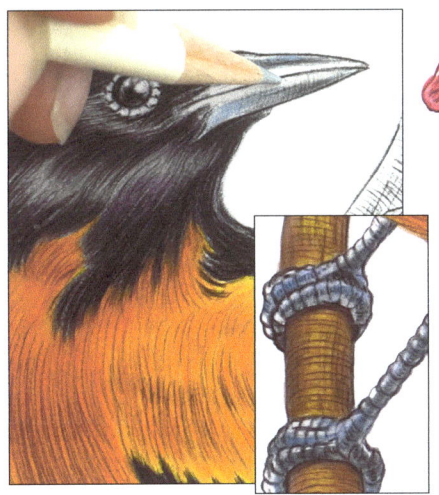

Step 4. Color the beak using (P-10) Pigeon Grey. For the Legs start with (DL-7) Jay Blue, leaving some areas white. Then color (P-10) Pigeon gray down the center to give the legs shape.

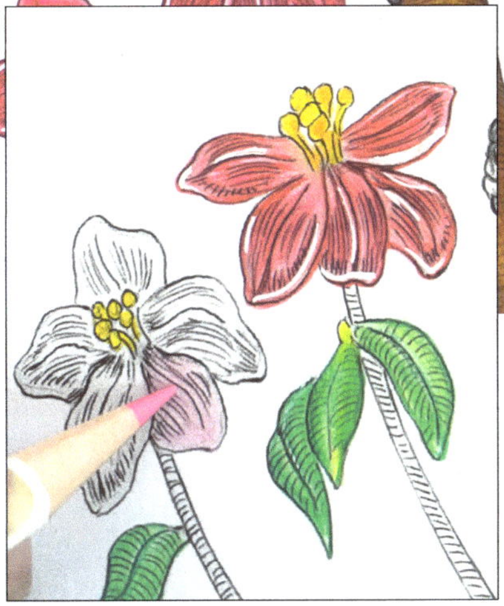

Step 5. Color the center of the flowers using (V-3) Dandelion and (V2) Tangerine Orange. Add a layer of (P-1) Orchid Pink to the flower petals and layer (P-2) Coral Pink and (V-1) Cherry Red on top. Add a few highlights using a white gel pen.

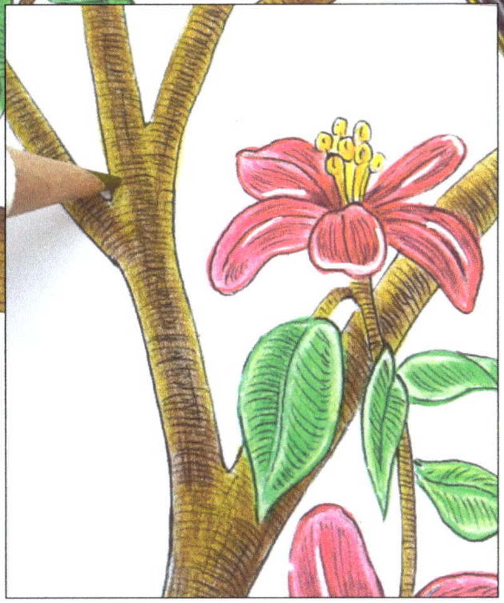

Step 6. Color the leaves by layering first (P-5) lettuce Green and then (V-5) Parrot Green around the edges. For the trunk color in the whole trunk using (D-2) Chestnut Brown and color down the center of each branch using (D-4) Maple Sugar.

Spreading Awareness through Coloring

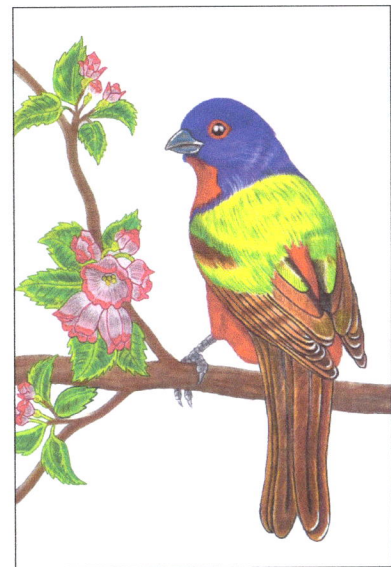

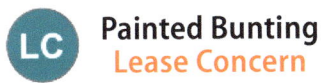 **Painted Bunting**
Lease Concern

I truly believe that raising awareness through the sharing of my artwork is a fantastic way to educate people about conservation. And coloring animals is a beautiful way to learn about them as you enjoy a relaxing and fun pastime. I am very happy to tell you that all of the song birds in this coloring book are list as "Least Concern" on the *International Union for Conservation of Nature's (IUCN)* conservation list. I think it's important to include the *(IUCN)* conservation list in my books so people understand the classifications more clearly. To the right is an overview of the IUCN's conservation list, which breaks animals' conservation statuses into several categories. Knowing what these categories mean and the animals that are included in them is extremely important. **Together through art we can change the world!**

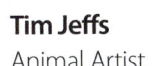

Tim Jeffs
Animal Artist

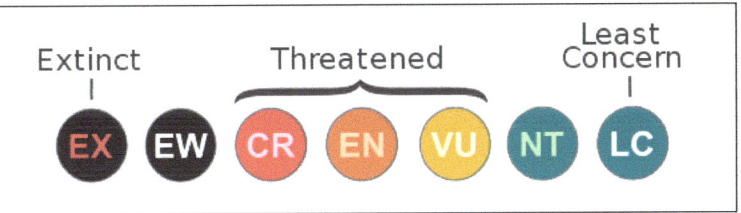

The list consists of 7 categories. From Least Concerned all the way to Extinct. Here are the definitions of each category:

- **LEAST CONCERN (LC):** A species that has been evaluated but not qualified for any other category on the list.

- **NEAR THREATENED (NT):** A species that may be considered threatened with extinction in the near future.

- **VULNERABLE (VU):** A species likely to become endangered unless the circumstances that are threatening its survival and reproduction improve.

- **ENDANGERED (EN):** A species that is considered very likely to become extinct.

- **CRITICALLY ENDANGERED (CR):** A species that is facing an extremely high risk of becoming extinct in the wild.

- **EXTINCT IN THE WILD (EW):** A species that is only known by living members kept in captivity or as a naturalized population outside its historic range due to massive habitat loss.

- **EXTINCT (EX):** A species that has been terminated.

Learn about the *Song* Birds

Before you start coloring, it's important to learn where the birds in this book live and to know their conservation status are all "Least Concern".

❱ American Goldfinch
A small North American bird it's range is from Canada to the Mexico. It benefits from human activity because it is attracted to bird feeders in residential areas.

❱ Baltimore Oriole
This bird is a common blackbird in eastern North America. It got it's name from the resemblance of the male's colors to the coat-of-arms of Lord Baltimore.

❱ Eurasian Blue Tit
A small passerine bird in the tit family. It is a non-migratory bird and is common throughout temperate Europe and western Palearctic.

❱ European Robin
Also know as the Robin redbreast it is found across Europe, east and western Siberia and south and North Africa.

❱ Green Headed Tanager
This bird is brightly-colored and lives in the Atlantic forest of south-eastern Brazil and far eastern Paraguay.

❱ Mountain Bluebird
Found in Mountainous areas of North America it is a small migratory thrush. Males are bright turquoise-blue and lighter underneath.

❱ Orange-Backed Troupial
It is found in Guyana, Brazil, Paraguay, and eastern Ecuador, Bolivia and Peru. They get their name Troupial from a the French word troupe or (troop) because the live in flocks..

❱ Painted Bunting
A species of cardinal native to southern North America. The males bright plumage on comes in the second year of life.

❱ Red Cardinal
It can be found in southeastern Canada, throughout the eastern United States, and south through Mexico, Belize and Guatemala. Once Prized as a pet it was banned as a cage bird in 1918,

❱ Scarlet Tanager
It range is from Canada to South America. Until recently it was place in the Tanager family, but it is now classified in the cardinal family.

❱ Song Thrush
Found across West Palearctic it winters in southern Europe, North Africa and the Middle East. It's distinctive song has repeated musical phrases.

❱ Violet-Backed Starling
Also know as the plum-colored starling or amethyst starling it lives in the woodlands and Savannah forests of sub-Saharan Africa.

❱ Western Meadowlark
Found in the grasslands across western and central North America. It's distinctive calls are described as watery or flute-like.

❱ Western Tanager
Found in the woods across western North America from the Mexico-U.S. border as far north as southern Alaska, they are the northernmost breeding tanager.

❱ Whiteheads Broadbill
Restricted to mountainous forests in northern Borneo, is named after the British explorer John Whitehead who studied the species in the 1800s.

SongBirds Index

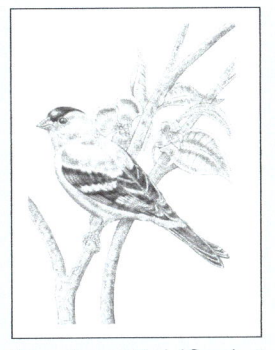
American Goldfinch 1

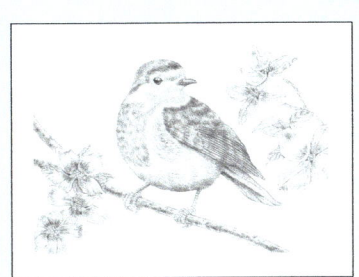
European Robin 4

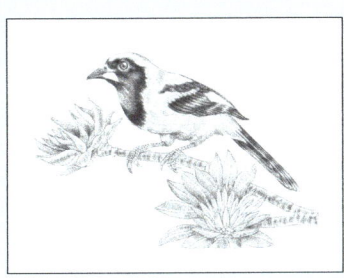
Orange-Back Troupial 7

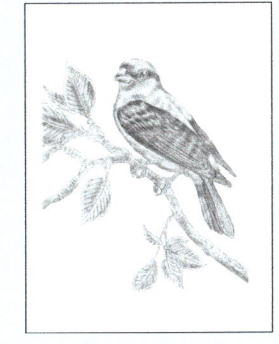
Scarlet Tanager 10

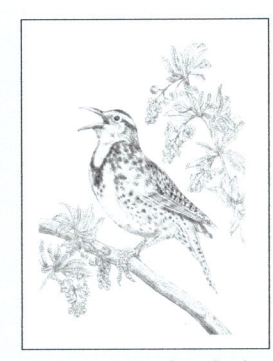
Western Meadowlark 13

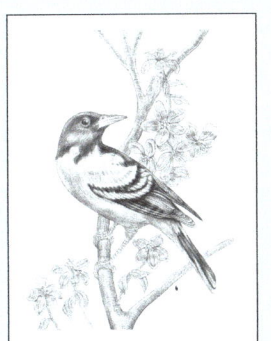
Baltimore Oriole 2

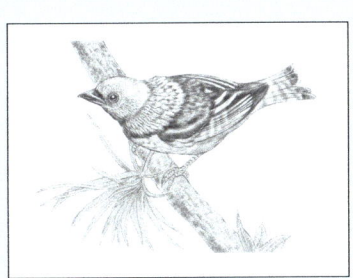
Green Headed Tanager 5

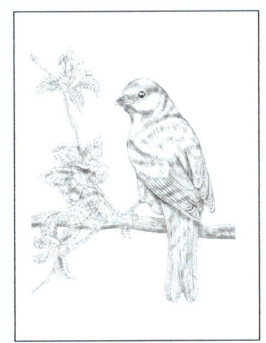
Painted Bunting 8

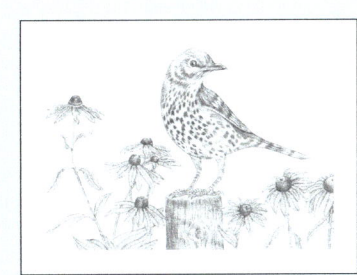
Song Thrush 11

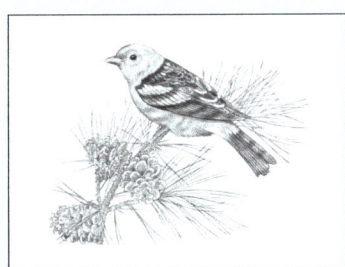
Western Tanager 14

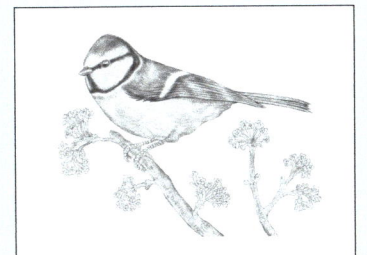
Eurasian Blue Tit 3

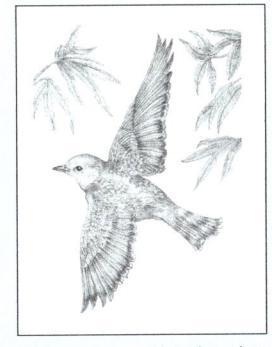
Mountain Bluebird 6

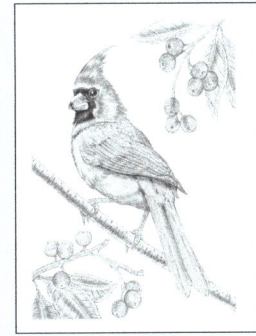
Red Cardinal 9

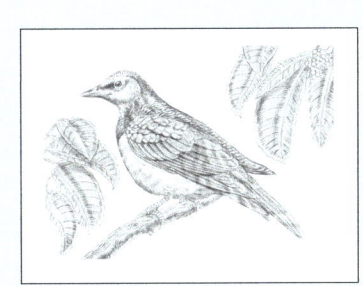
Violet Backed Starling 12

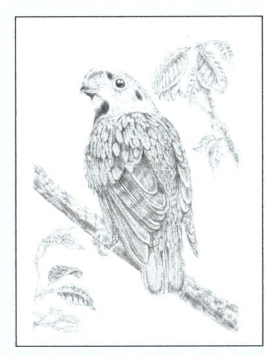
Whiteheads Broadbill 15

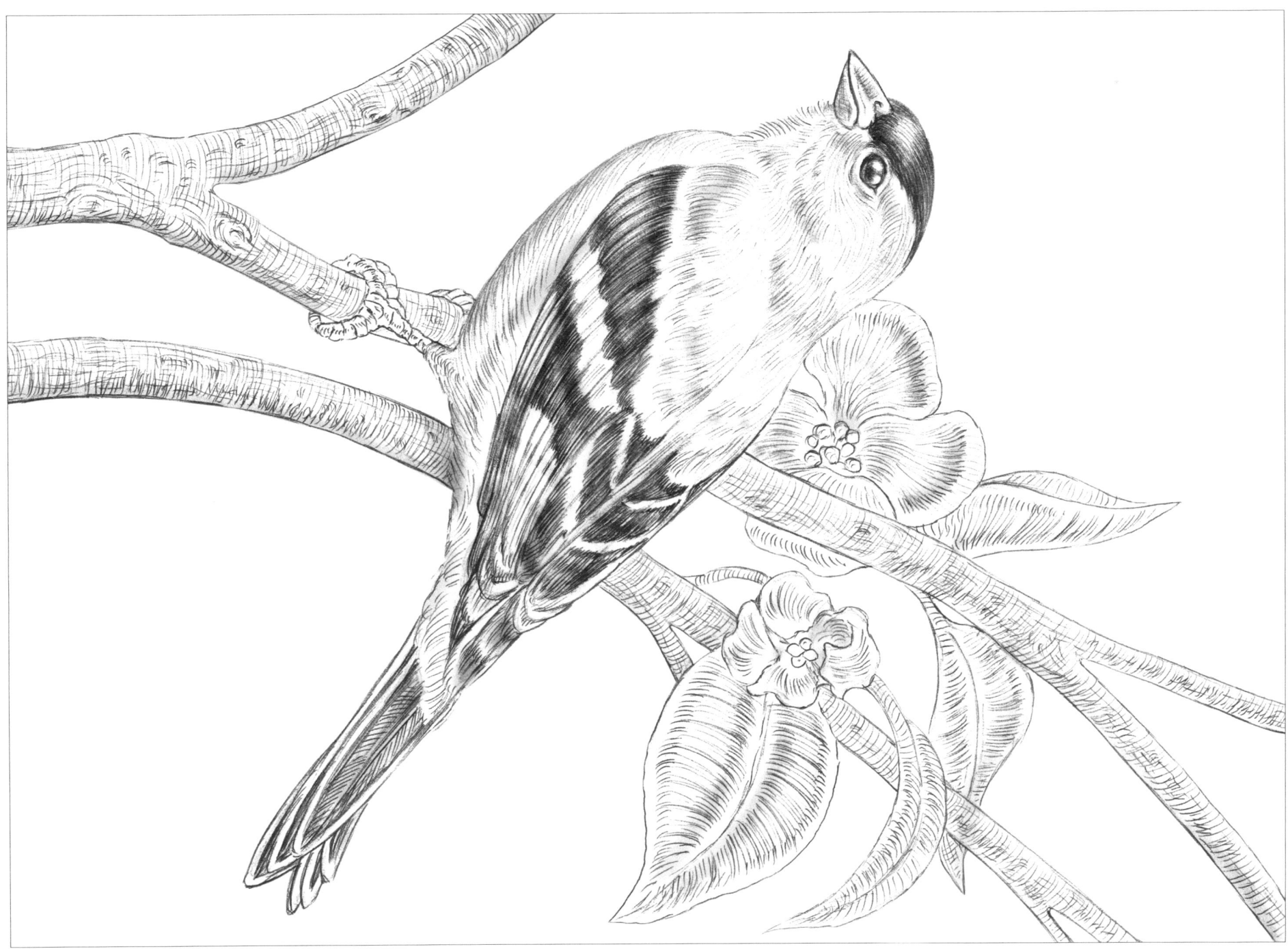

American Goldfinch

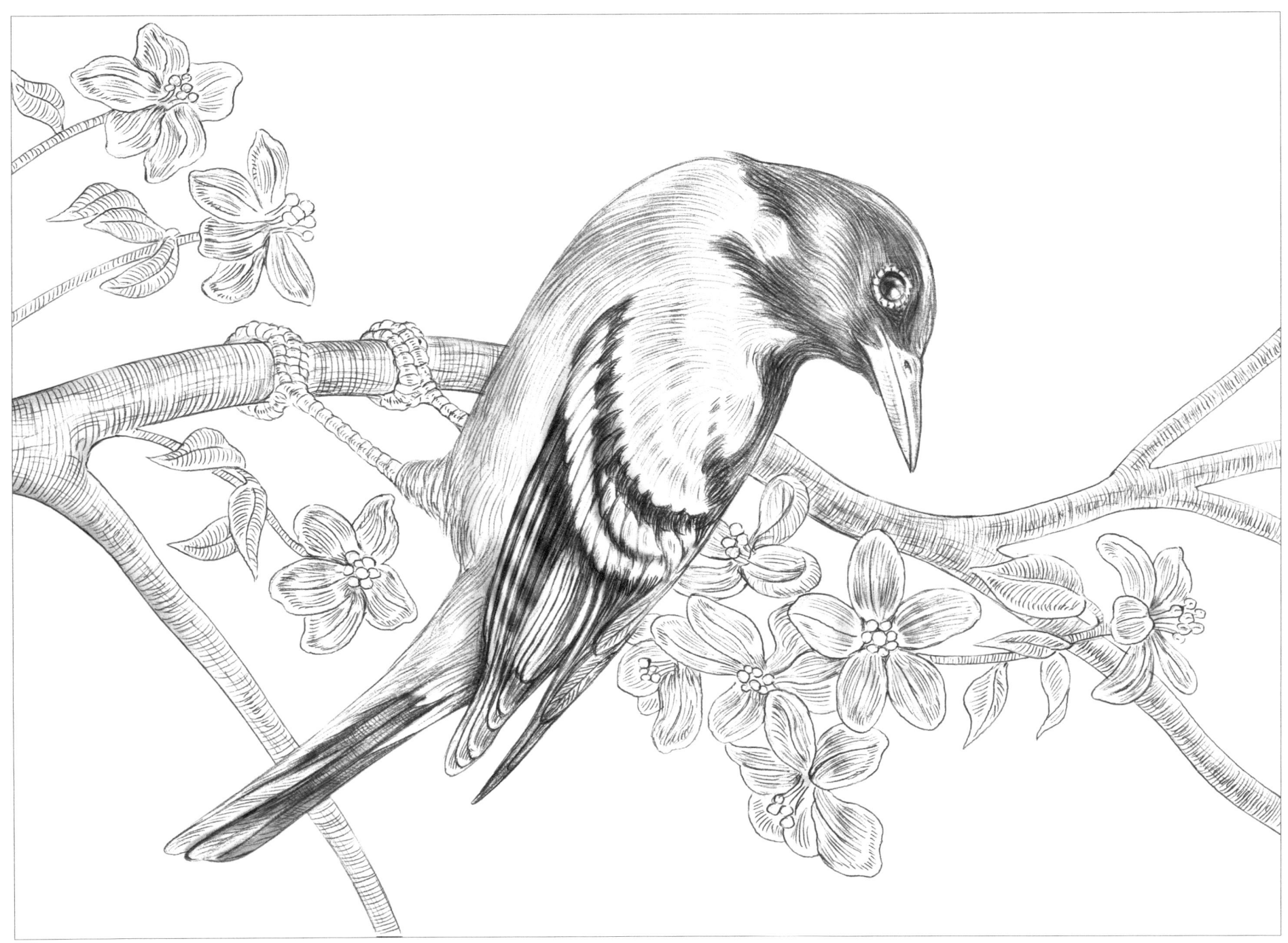

Baltimore Oriole

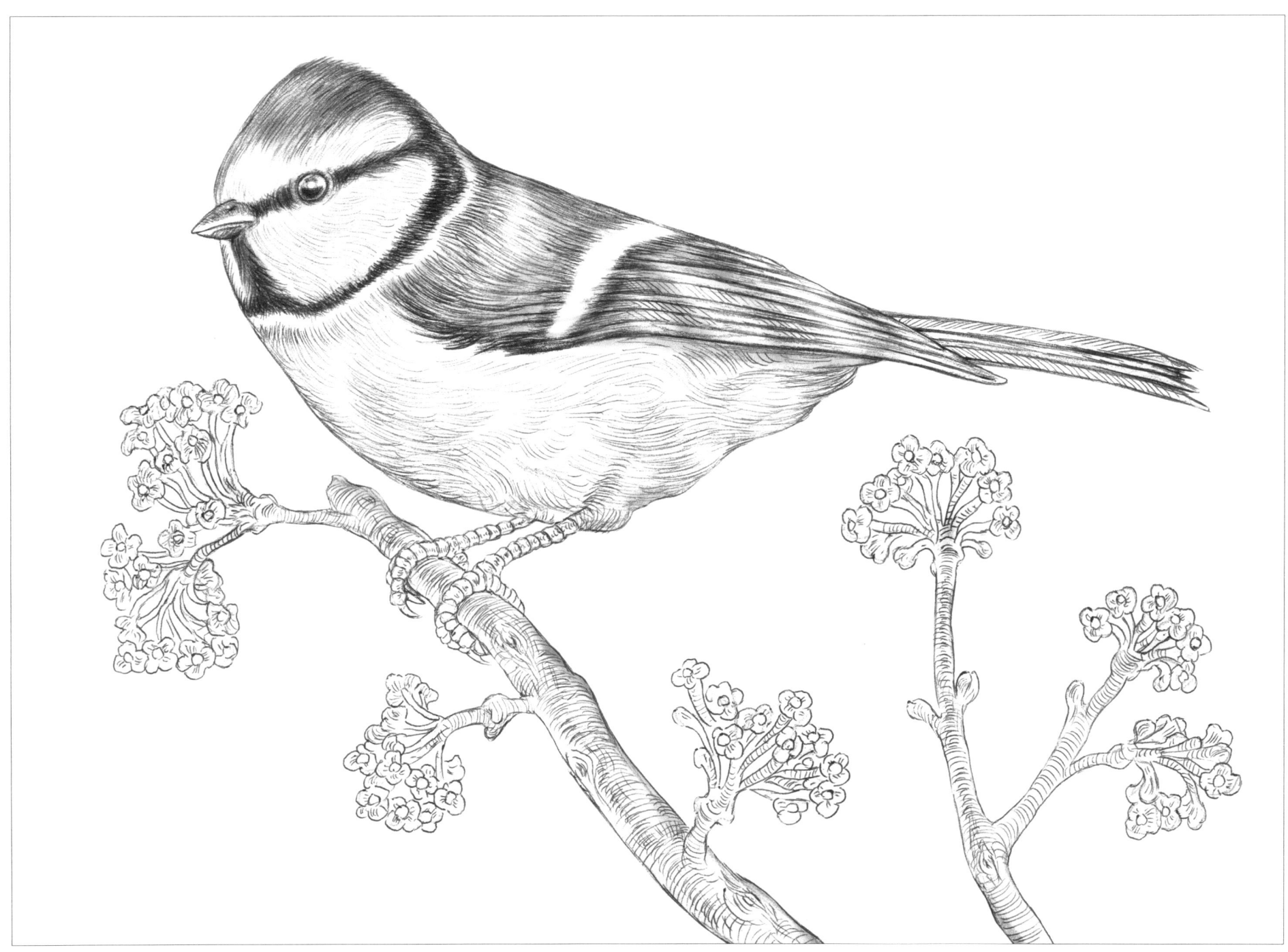

Eurasian Blue Tit

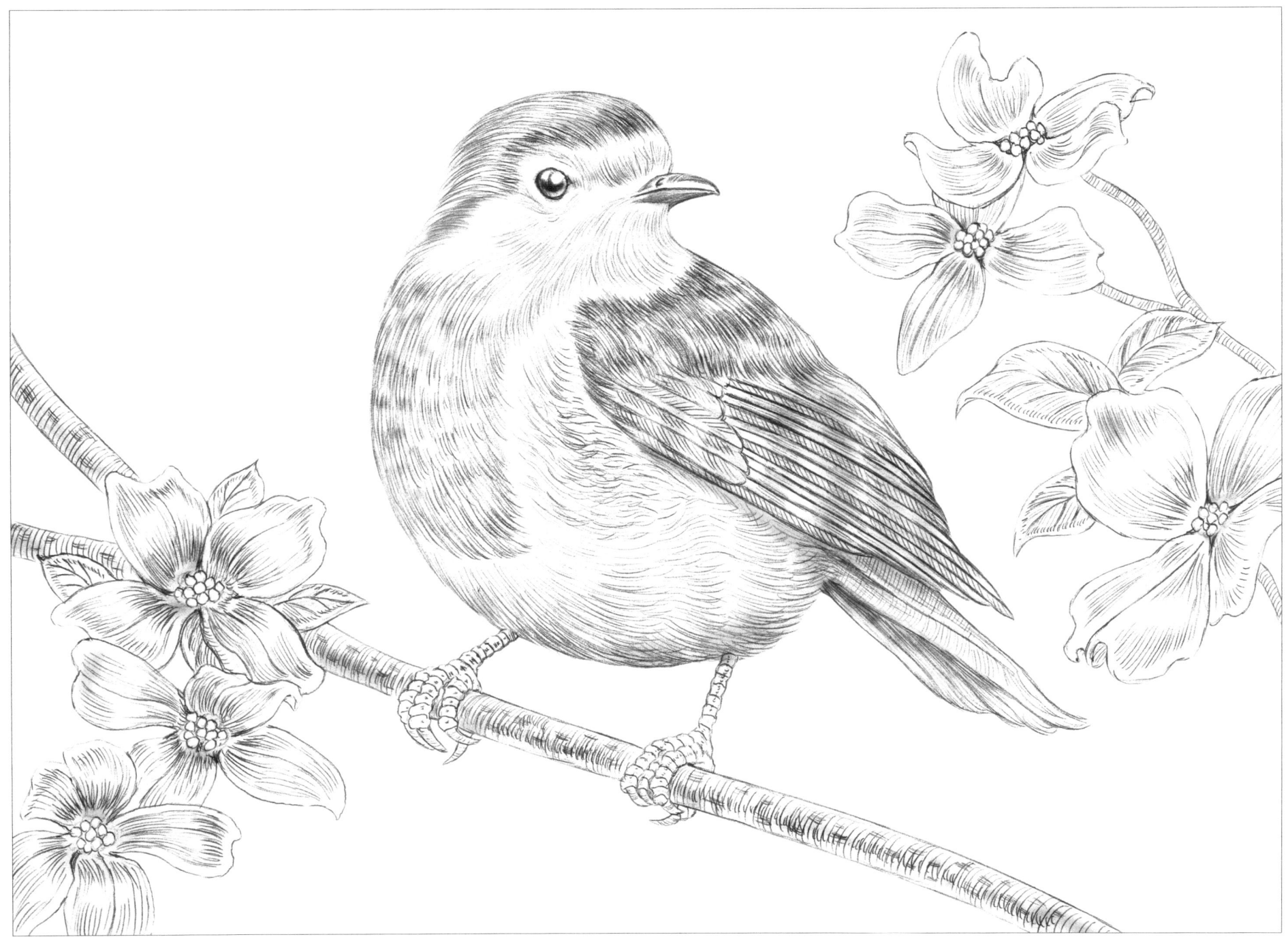

European Robin

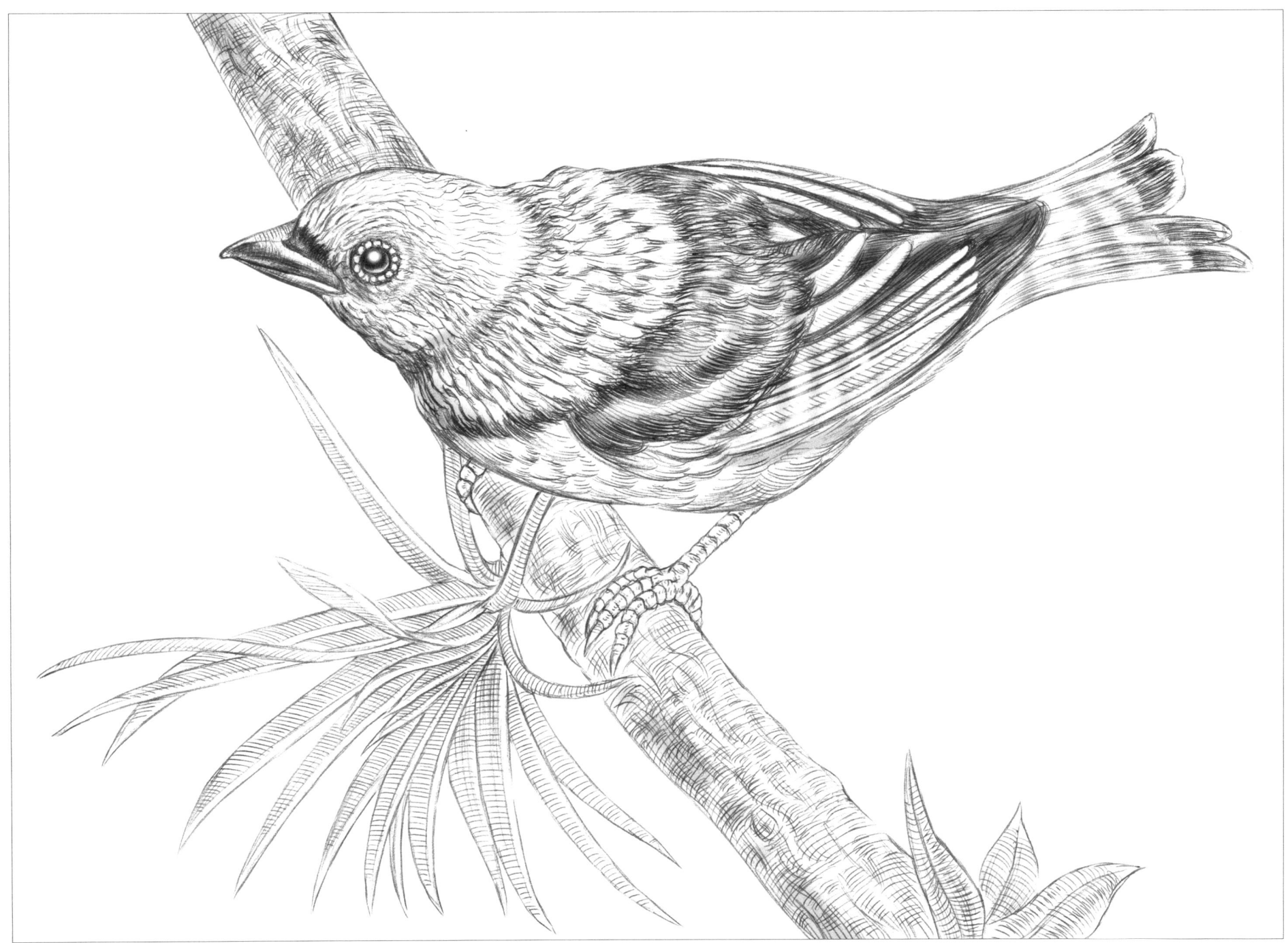

Green Headed Tanager

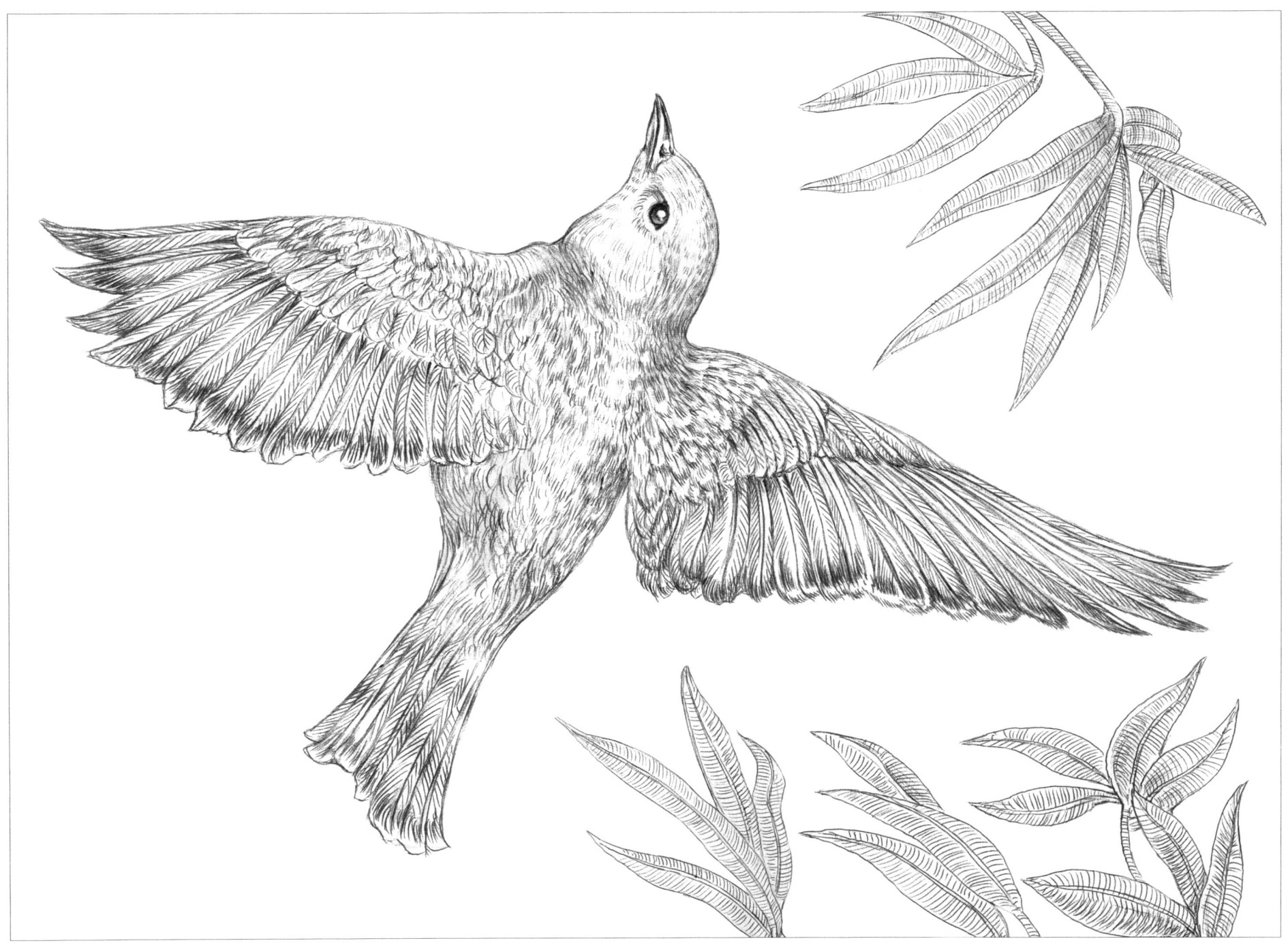

Mountain Bluebird

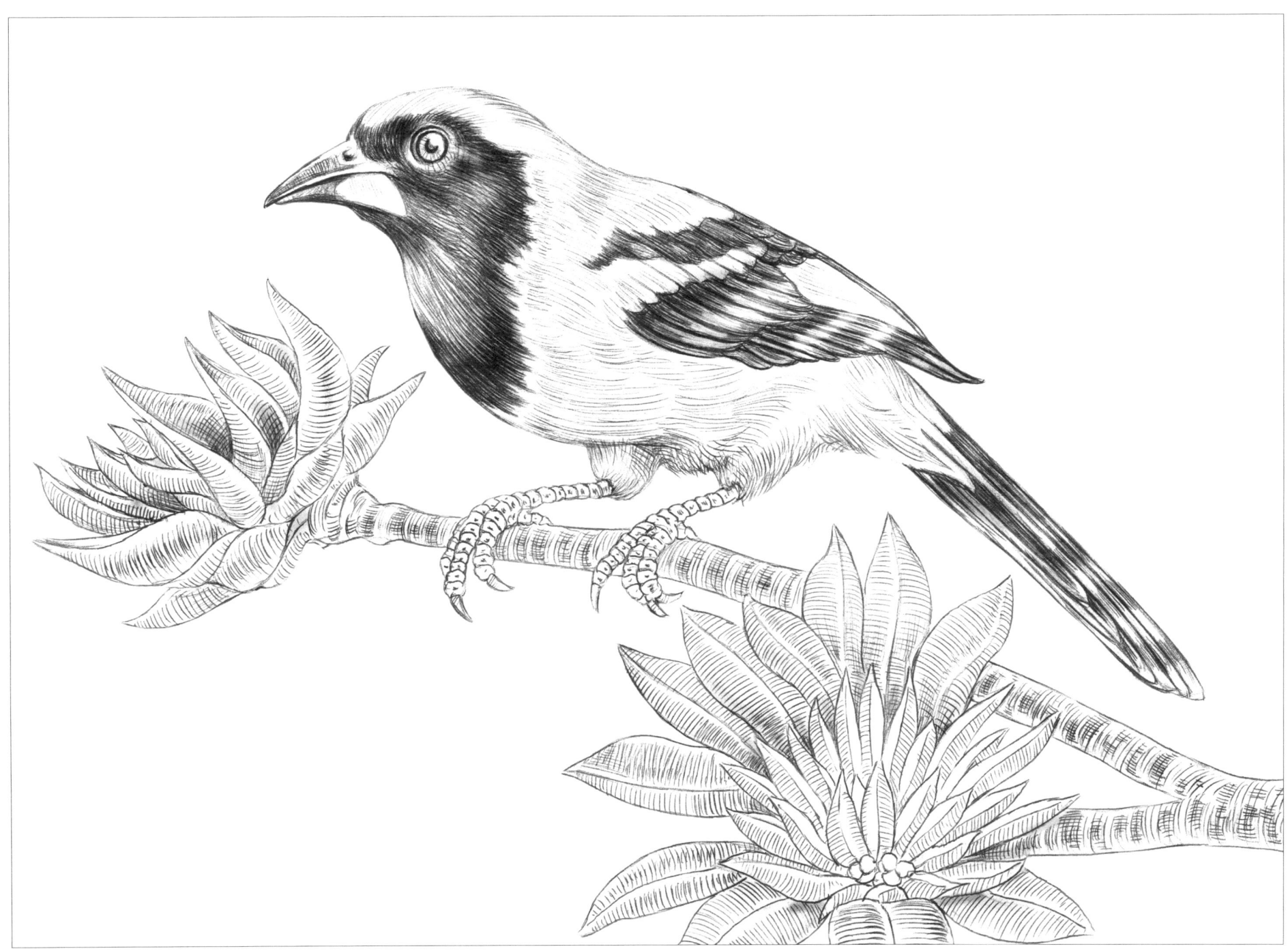

Orange-Back Troupial

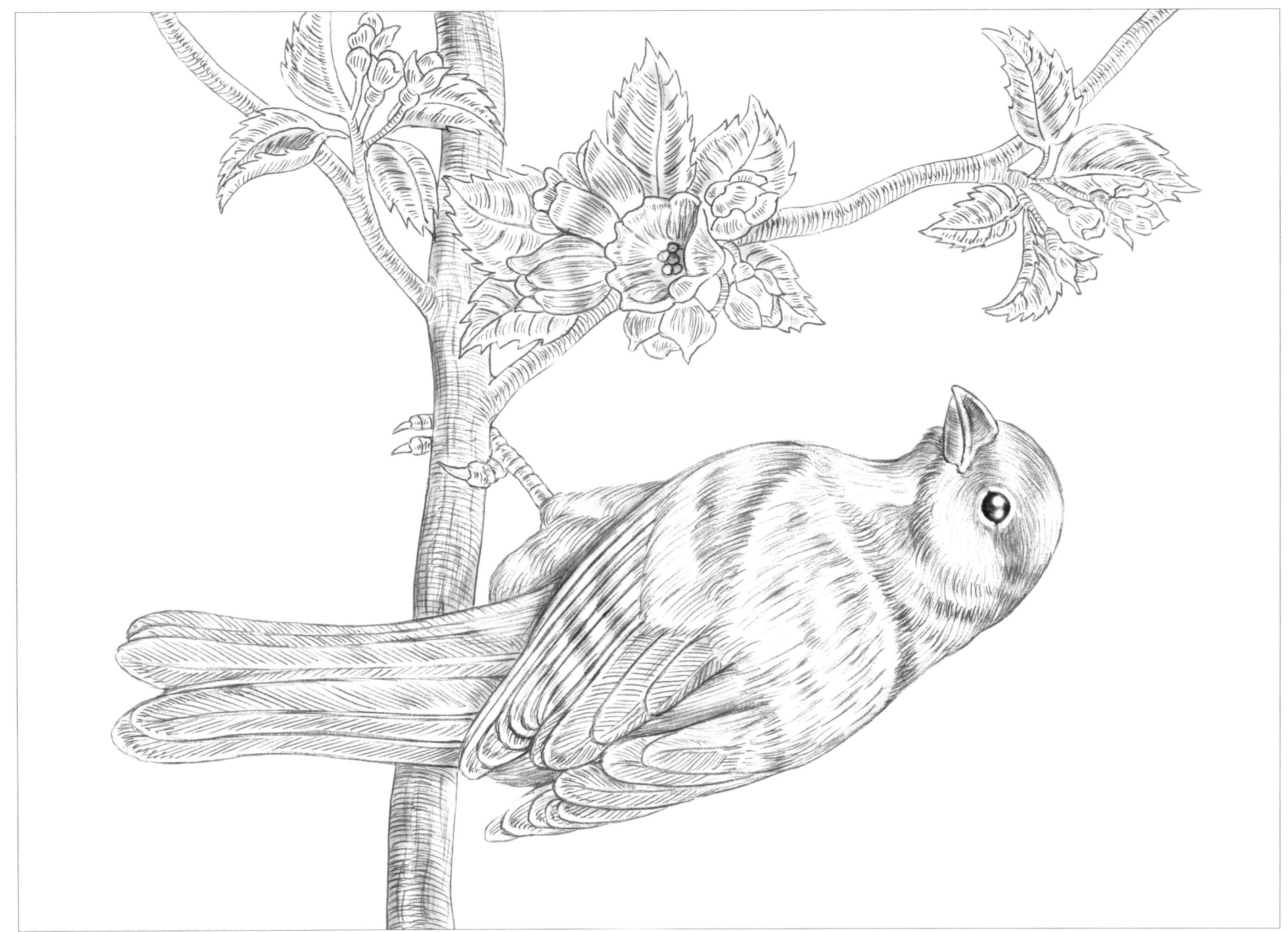

Painted Bunting

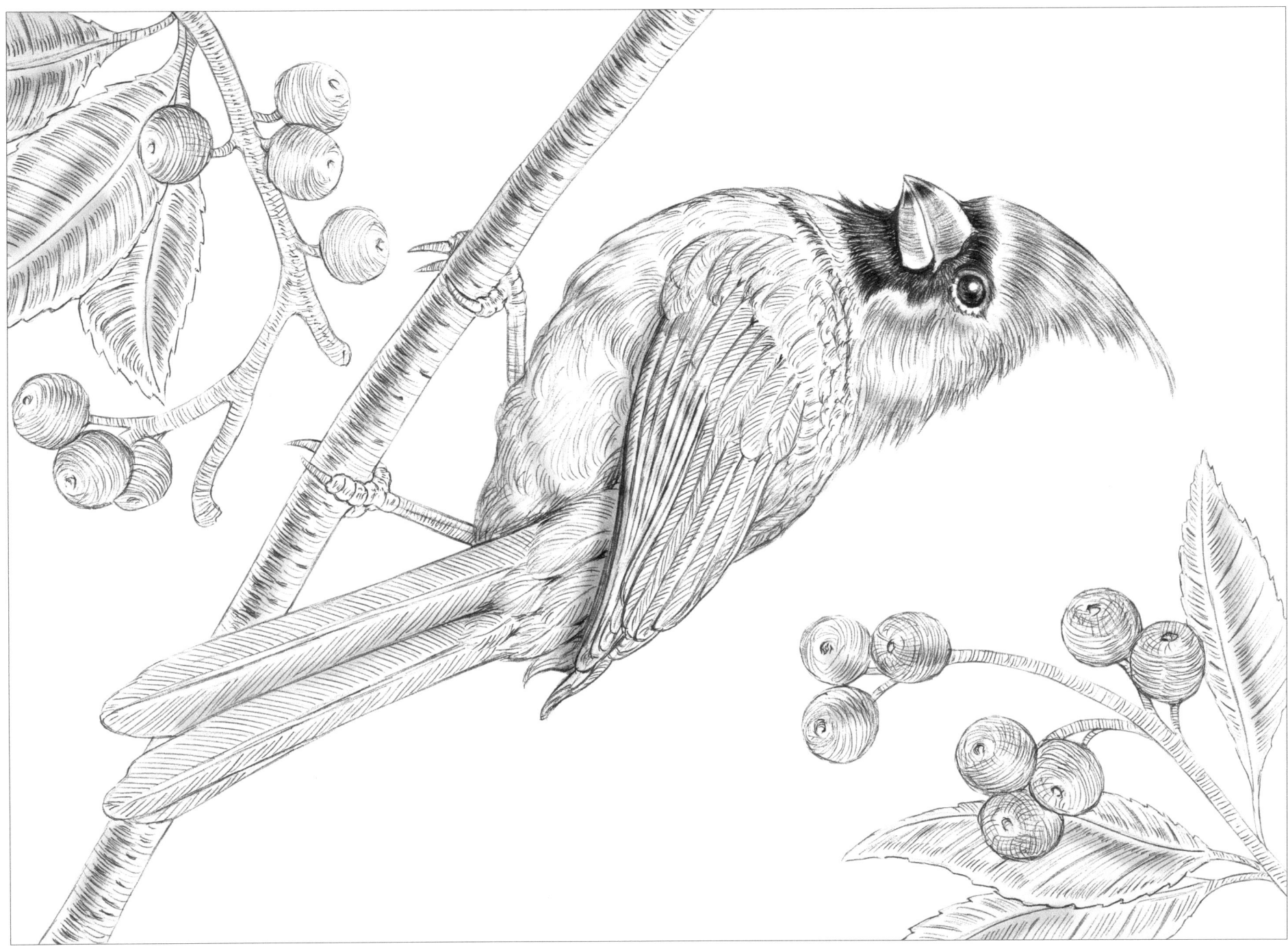

Red Cardinal

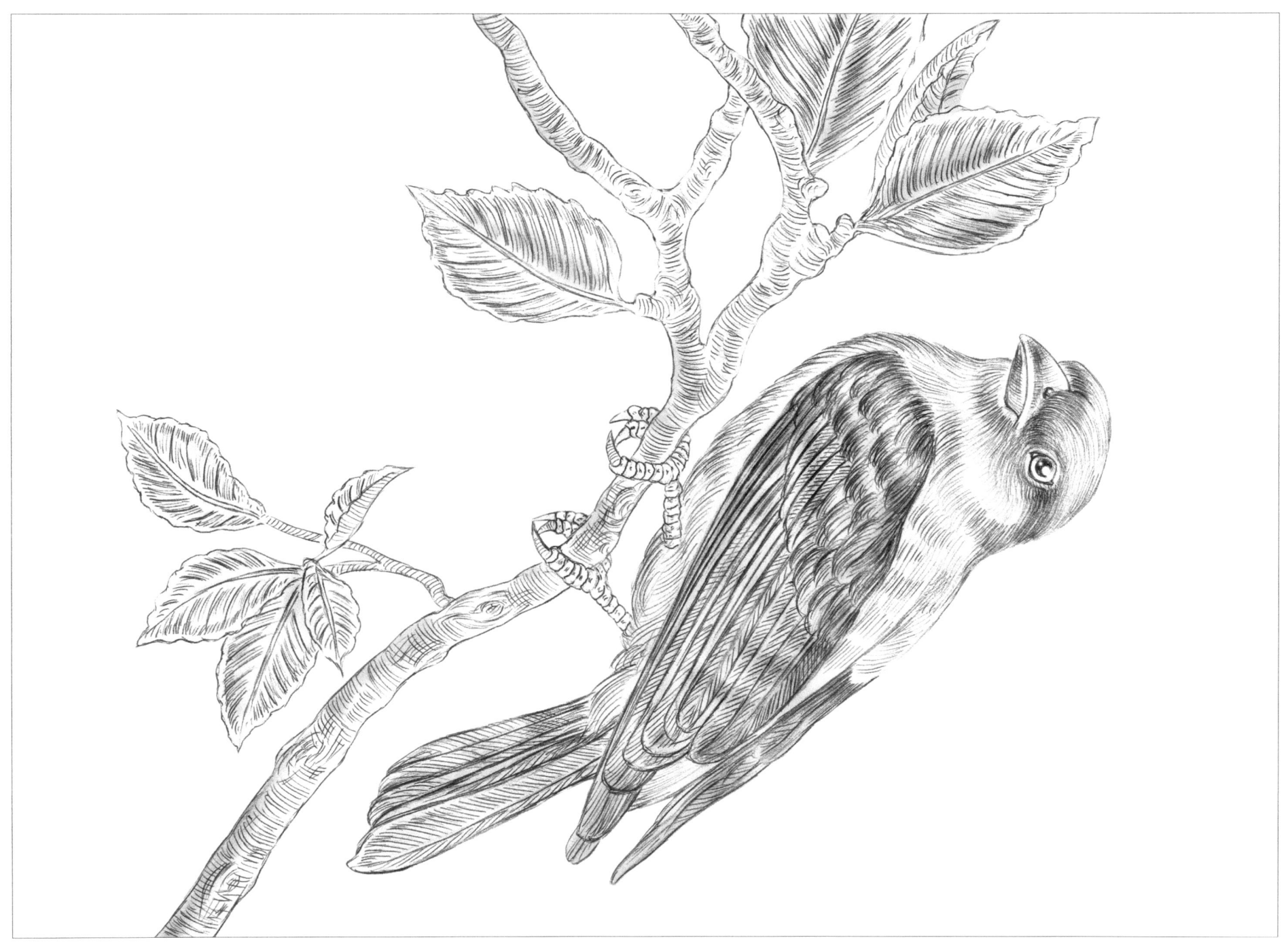

Scarlet Tanager

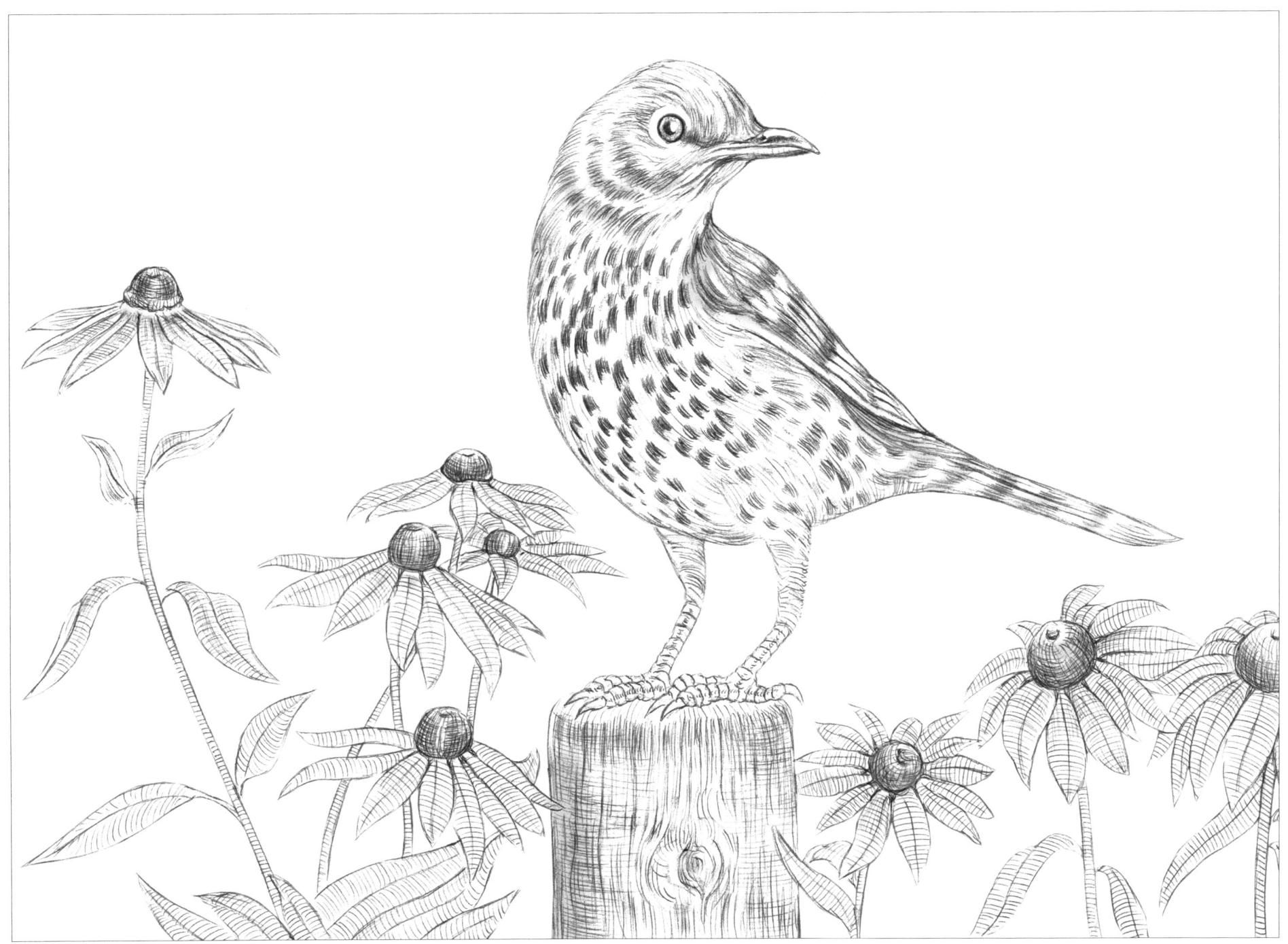

Song Thrush

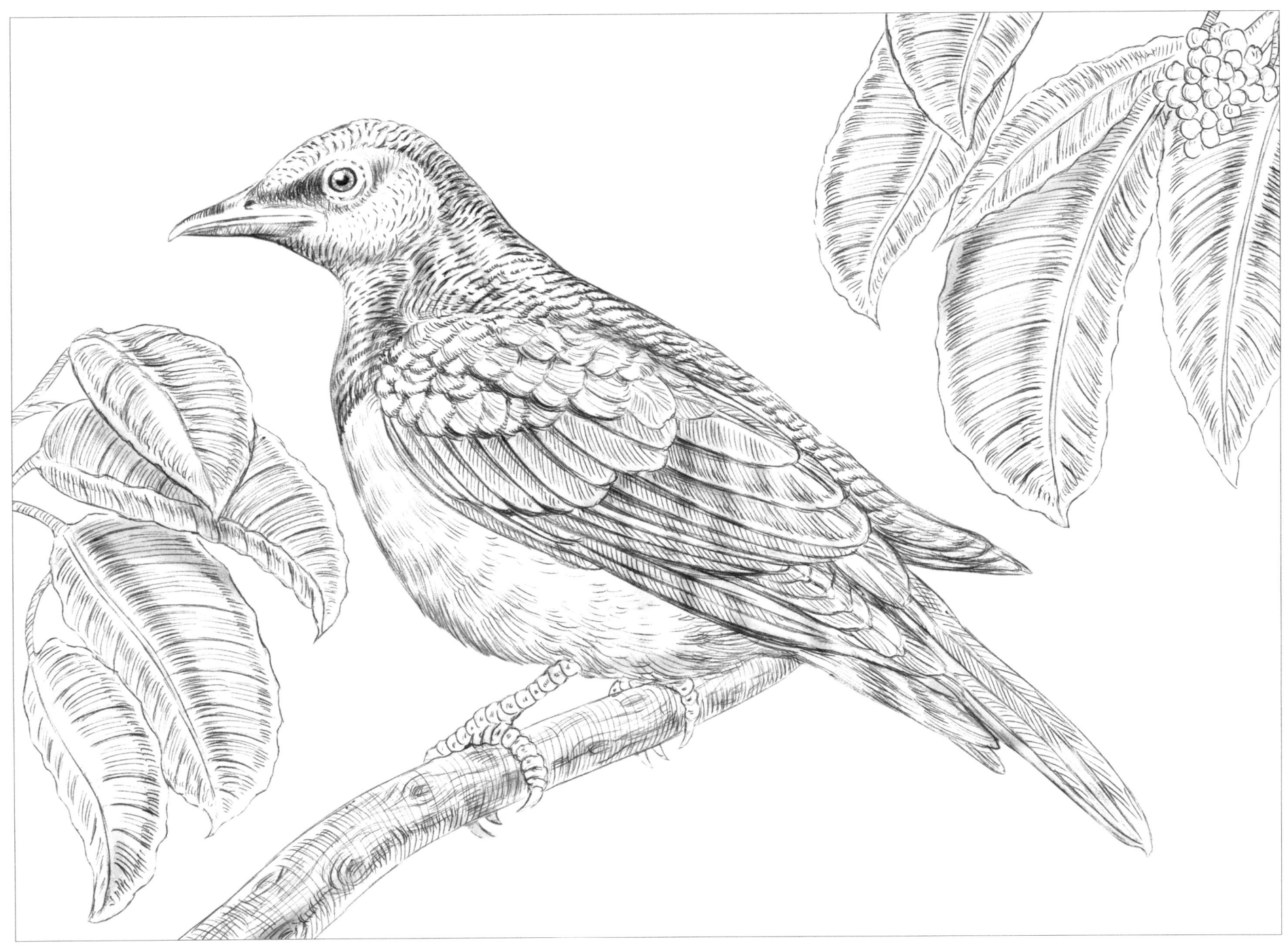

Violet-Backed Starling

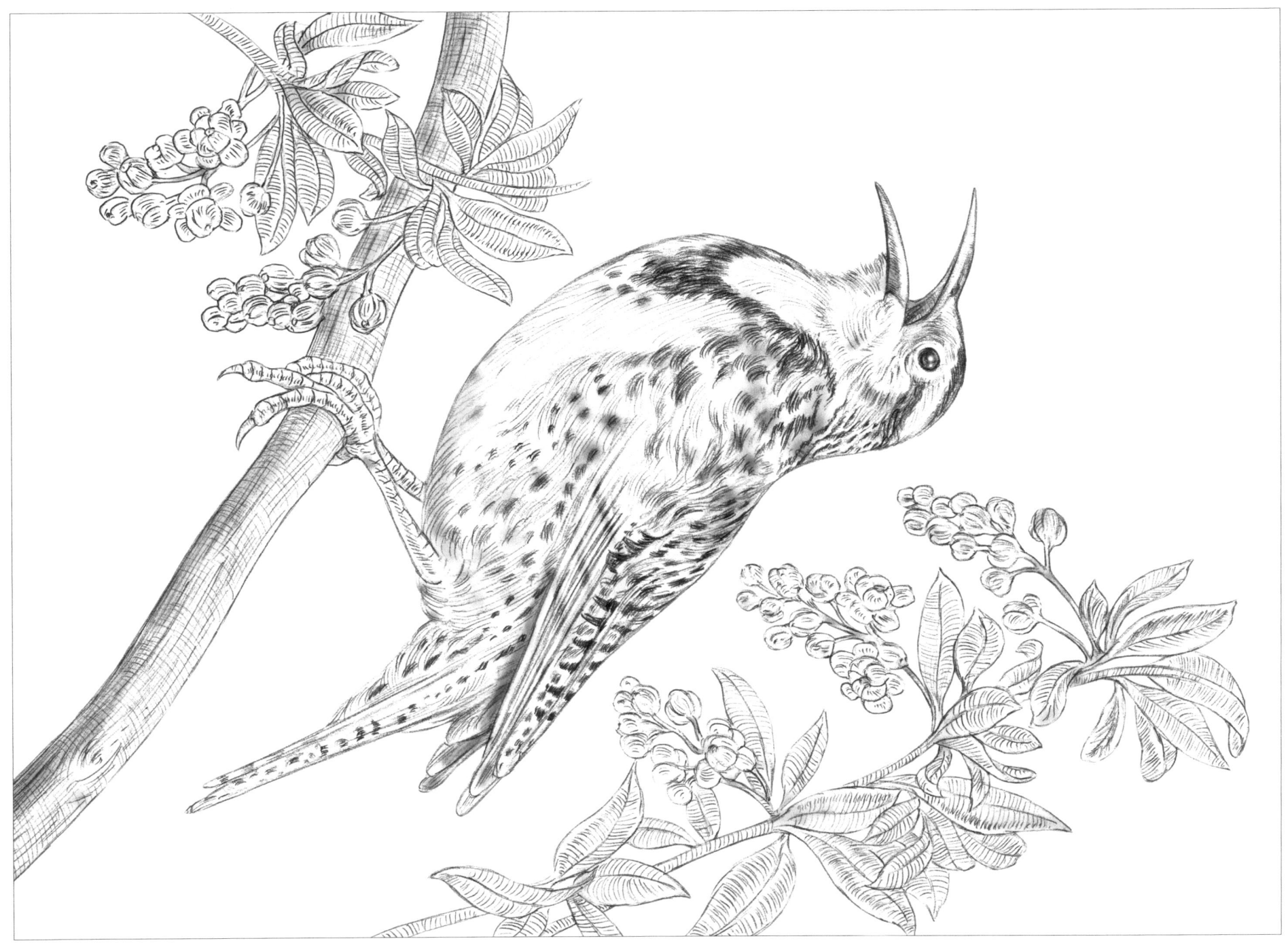

Western Meadowlark

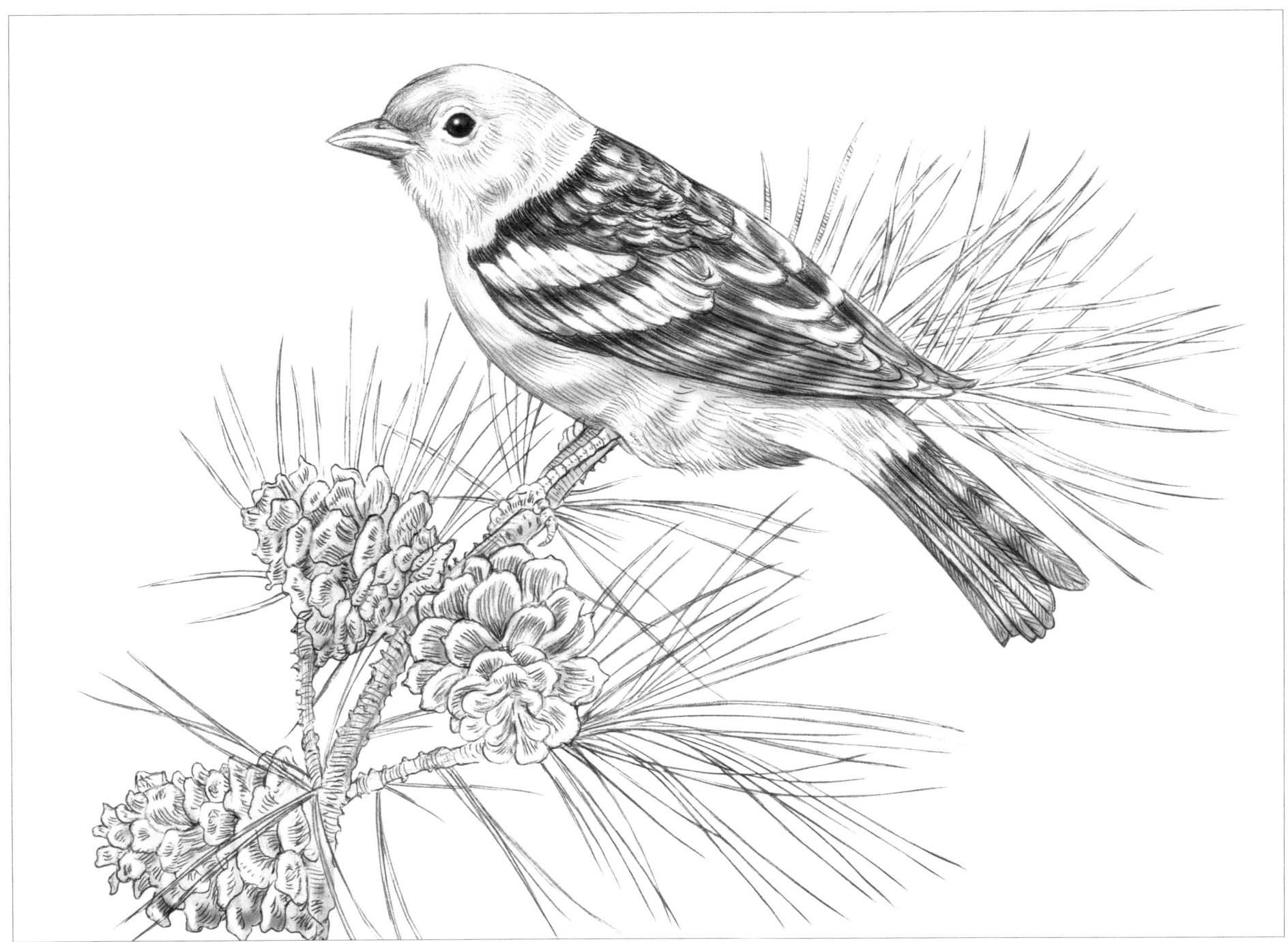
Western Tanager

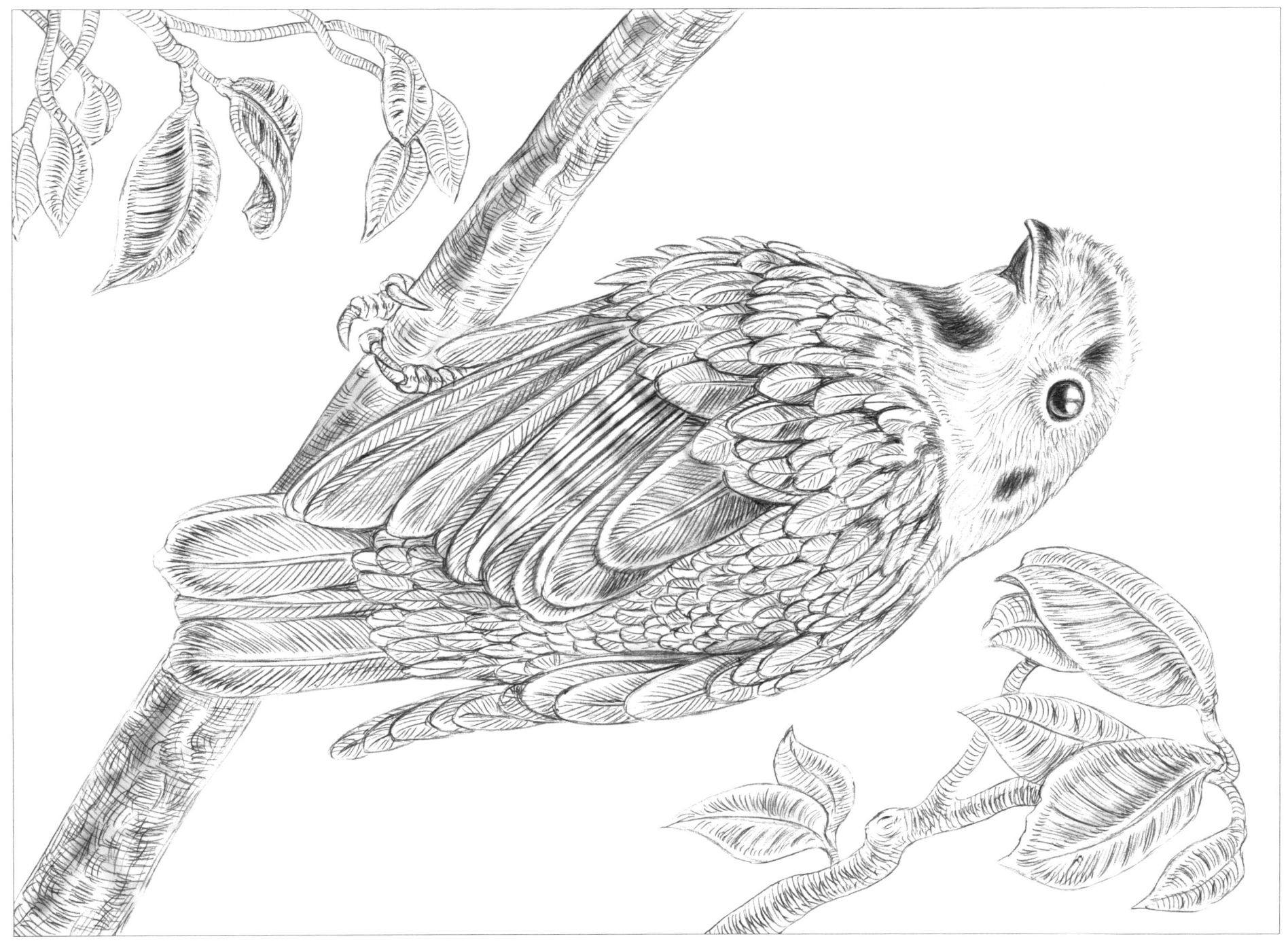

Whiteheads Broadbill

Tim Jeffs is a New York City based artist and illustrator who has been creating dynamic artwork for over 25 years. Animals are a favorite subject matter of his, along with the complex and intricate details these creatures possess. *"The incredible diversity and complexity of animals has always intrigued me. They offer endless pleasure to look and marvel upon. In every drawing I try to capture the unique quality of each particular animal. I hope you enjoy my perspective, love and admiration of these incredible creatures."*

Visit my website for prints, digital coloring books and coloring lessons:

www.TimJeffsArt.com

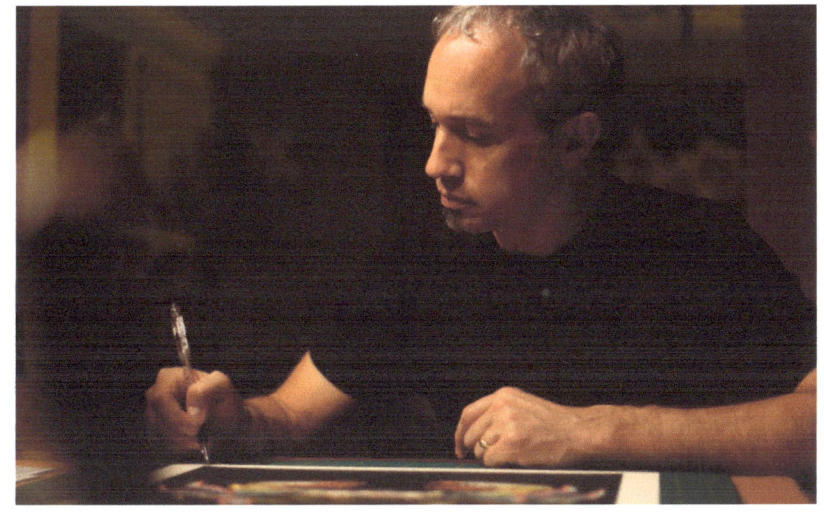

Discover the full line of Tim Jeffs' Published Coloring Books

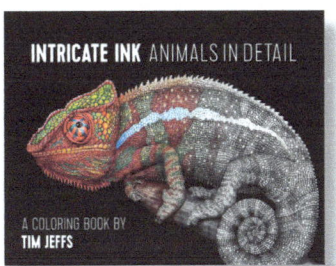 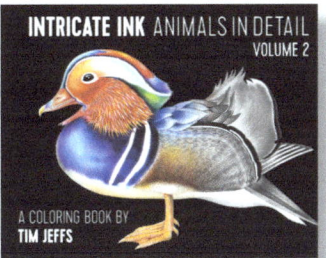 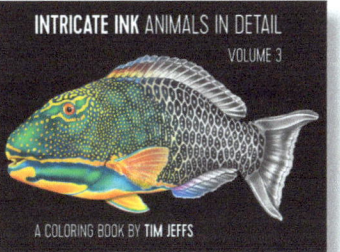 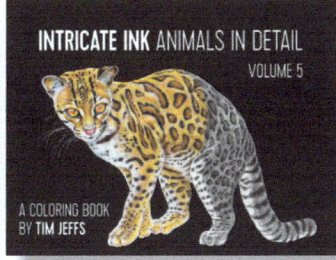 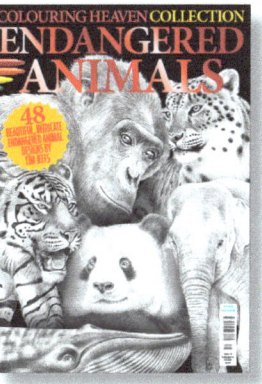

Intricate Ink Animals In Detail Volume 1, 2 3 and 5 Available at:
Pomegranate.com
Amazon.com
Bookdepository.com

**Colouring Heaven Collection
Endangered Animals**
Available at: Colouringheaven.com

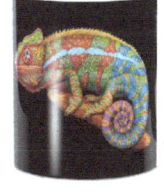

Discover Tim Jeffs' Merchandise

Etsy Shop
www.etsy.com/shop/TimJeffsArt

Society6 Shop
www.society6.com/TimJeffsArt

Redbubble Shop
TimJeffsArt.redbubble.com

Vsual Print Shop
https://vsual.co/shop/tim-jeffs-art

Discover the full line of Tim Jeffs Digital Coloring Books at:
www.TimJeffsArt.com

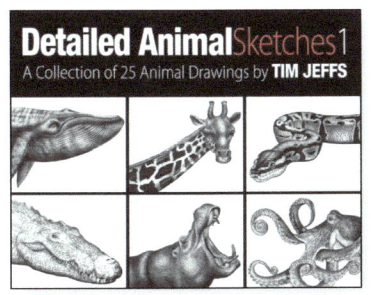
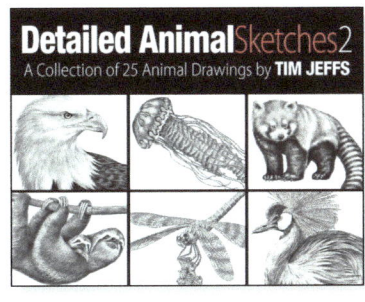
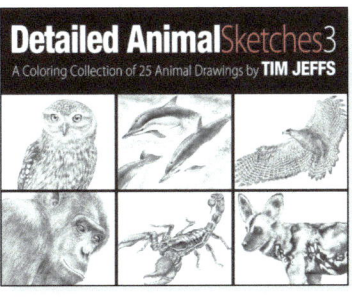
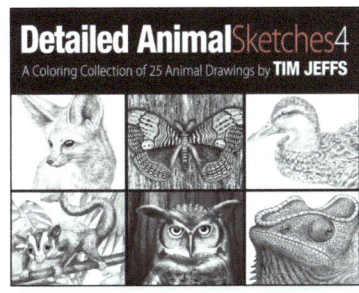
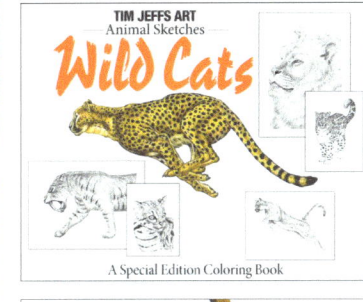
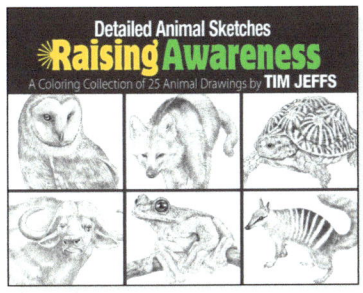
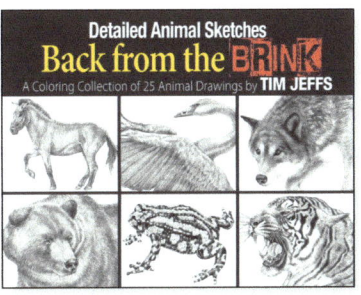
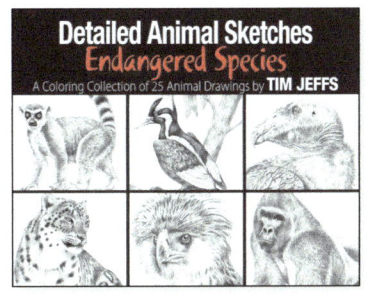
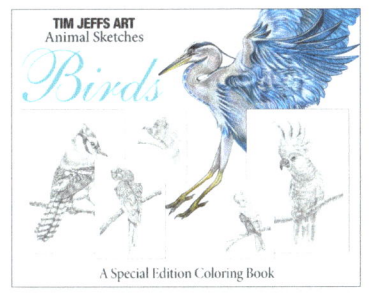
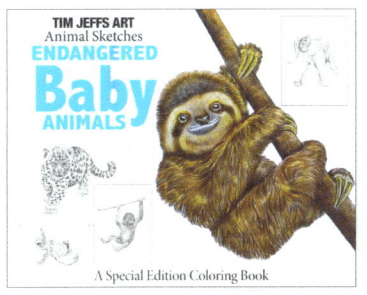

And Coloring Lessons

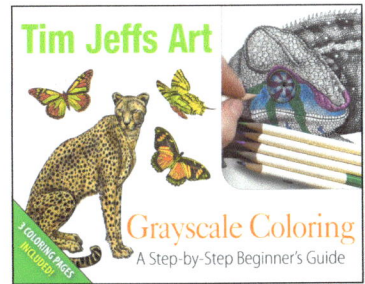
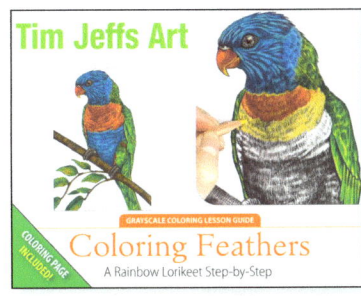
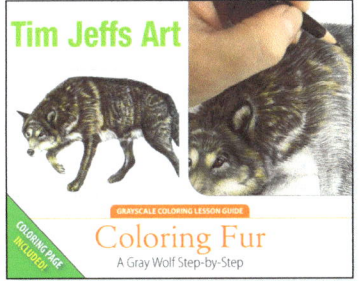
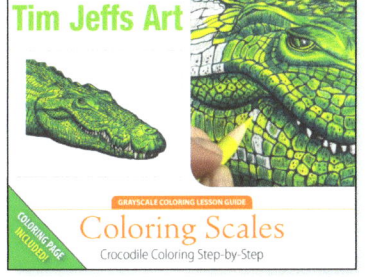
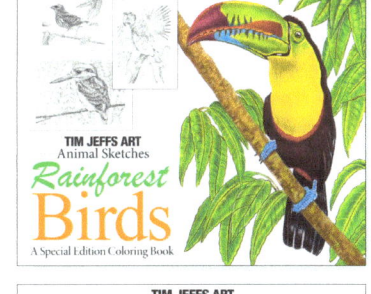
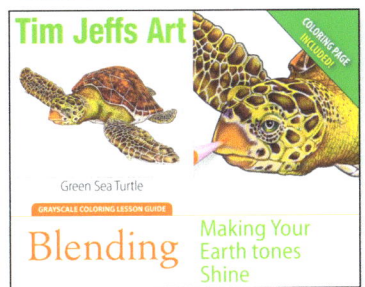
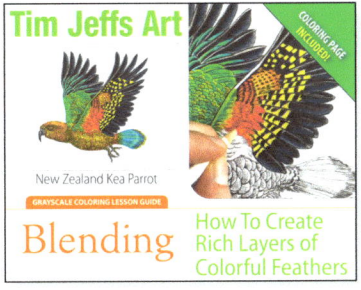
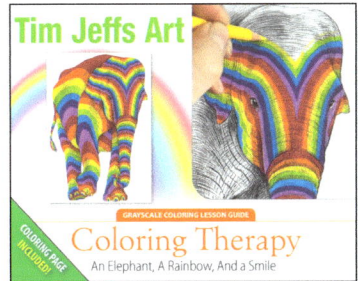
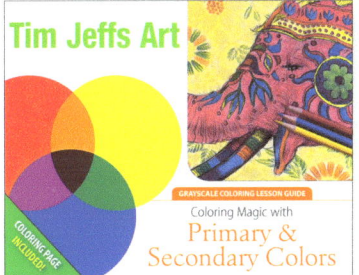
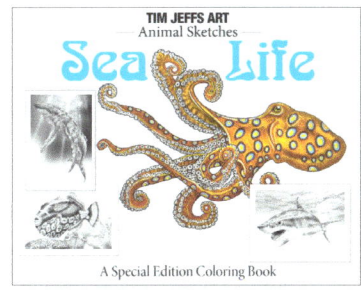

TIM JEFFS ART Online Resources

Share Your Creativity with the World!

Join the ever-expanding coloring group of animal lovers who inspire each other through their colorings of the animals from Tim's books and lessons. With thousands of members from all around the world, Tim's Facebook group "Intricate Ink Coloring Group" is a creative and safe space where everyone is welcome. Jo Warren, the groups all-inspiring administrator will welcome you in with open arms and is there to encourage everyone to just have fun no matter your coloring skill level. Come join, we can't wait to have you as a member! Join Tim's Facebook Coloring Group at:

www.facebook.com/groups/intricateink

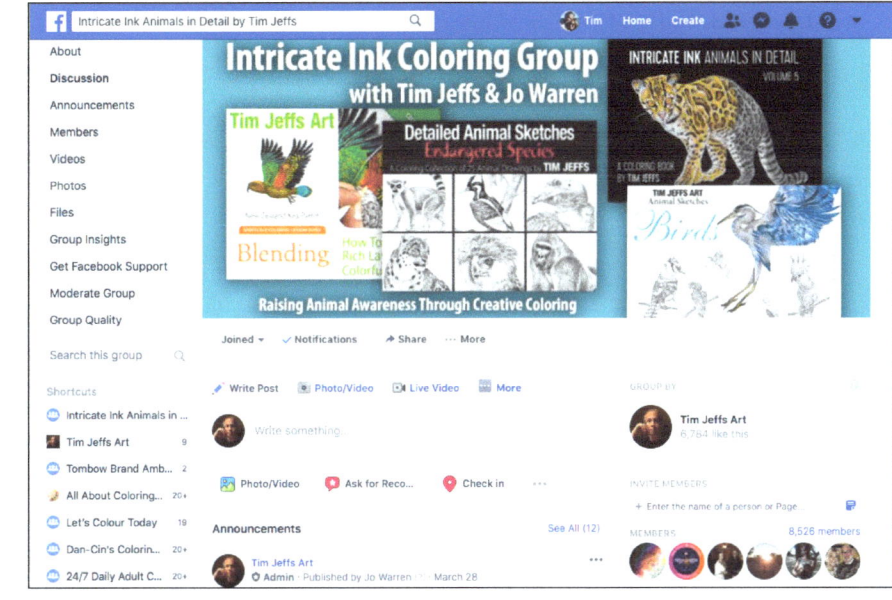

Visit the Home of Tim Jeffs Art

TimJeffsArt.com is my home on the web where I display all of my work and various projects. I hope you can stop by for a visit! You'll find my new shop where signed and unsigned prints of all of my animal drawings are available to purchase, along with the complete library of my digital download coloring books and grayscale coloring lessons. In the conservation section, you can see the projects that I am very proud of. Using my art to preserve wildlife is so important to me.

www.TimJeffsArt.com

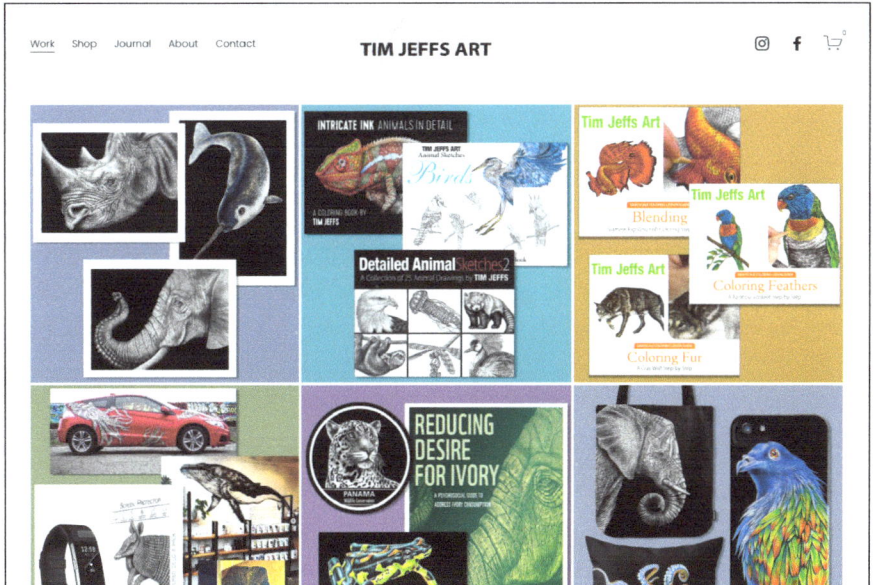

www.ingramcontent.com/pod-product-compliance
Lightning Source LLC
Chambersburg PA
CBHW051222220526
45473CB00003B/1129